Cedar Mill & Bethany
Community Libraries
library.cedarmill.org

WITHDRAWN
JUL 2021
CEDAR MILL LIBRARY

D1442946

THE
SELF-CARE
KIT FOR
STRESSED-OUT
TEENS

Frankie Young

THE SELF-CARE KIT FOR STRESSED-OUT TEENS

Copyright © Summersdale Publishers Ltd, 2021

With research and text by Anna Martin

All rights reserved.

No part of this book may be reproduced by any means, nor transmitted, nor translated into a machine language, without the written permission of the publishers.

Condition of Sale
This book is sold subject to the condition that it shall not, by way of trade or otherwise, be lent, resold, hired out or otherwise circulated in any form of binding or cover other than that in which it is published and without a similar condition including this condition being imposed on the subsequent purchaser.

An Hachette UK Company
www.hachette.co.uk

Vie Books, an imprint of Summersdale Publishers Ltd
Part of Octopus Publishing Group Limited
Carmelite House
50 Victoria Embankment
LONDON
EC4Y 0DZ
UK

www.summersdale.com

Printed and bound in China

ISBN: 978-1-78783-688-4

Substantial discounts on bulk quantities of Summersdale books are available to corporations, professional associations and other organisations. For details contact general enquiries: telephone: +44 (0) 1243 771107 or email: enquiries@summersdale.com.

The author and the publisher cannot accept responsibility for any misuse or misunderstanding of any information contained herein, or any loss, damage or injury, be it health, financial or otherwise, suffered by any individual or group acting upon or relying on information contained herein. None of the views or suggestions in this book are intended to replace medical opinion from a doctor. If you have concerns about your physical or mental health, please seek professional advice.

CONTENTS

HELLO!

Let's start at the beginning. Who bought you this book? Let's take a wild guess that it was your parent or a caring figure – maybe even a grandparent? The fact you've even dared to look inside the book is impressive! Maybe it has been at the bottom of the gift pile, or somewhere amid the chaos on your bedroom floor, or among the things shoved beneath your bed. Even more impressive is if you bought this for yourself; that is dedication and you should be proud. Hopefully this book is worth the anxiety you felt as you took it to the till or clicked buy.

So, you're a teenager. You've now reached the time of exams, new experiences and pubes! Are you prepared? No? Growing up is hard, isn't it? But the good thing is, everyone does it – even your parents were teenagers once (the horror!) – and this little guide offers simple ways to navigate these years smoothly. Teenage life will stretch you in more ways than you could ever have imagined, as well as being an exciting time, as thoughts turn to your future, new relationships and new experiences in the midst of exam pressure and big questions about identity, beliefs and discovering what makes you tick. This heady mix can often feel like a bit too much to handle, and that's where introducing self-care into your daily life can help.

WHAT IS SELF-CARE?

Well, it's self-explanatory; it's caring for yourself, which is a necessity – and that's not just brushing your teeth, it's about looking after yourself in the midst of the pressures of school, getting enough sleep (stop going to bed at 3 a.m., I see you) and being alert to when your mental, physical or emotional well-being is out of kilter. It's about acting upon all these things, so that you can be your best self.

Let's be clear about self-care from the start: it doesn't just involve pampering (although that can be a fun part of it). Self-care covers all manner of things, including eating healthily, getting enough sleep, having good friends to call upon, keeping fit, taking time out to pause when things get hectic and ultimately being able to tune in to your needs and respond to them.

CHAPTER 1:

PUT YOURSELF FIRST!

CARING FOR MYSELF IS NOT
SELF-INDULGENT; CARING
FOR MYSELF IS AN
ACT OF SURVIVAL.

Audre Lorde

In this chapter we're going to look at acts of kindness to yourself, such as saying no to things that drain your happiness, allowing yourself downtime in the midst of a busy life filled with with school, family and social responsibilities, and, ultimately, working on being your own best friend.

When you prioritize yourself, you are not being selfish; you are simply looking at yourself as you are right now – not projecting who you will be in the future – and addressing your present needs so that you can be completely engaged in your life and enjoy it to the full.

Ready?

LOOK OUT FOR YOURSELF

Self-care is all about YOU and caring for YOU. It doesn't mean that you can't be caring to others, too. Think of it like this: if you are drained of energy or feeling sad and low, you will not be able to be your best self, which will impact in a negative way on those around you. Investing time, energy and care in YOU will leave you with more reserves of energy to invest in the people and things that are most important to you. It's simple, when you think about it.

DO I DESERVE SELF-CARE?

Woah there! Remember this: SELF-CARE IS UNCONDITIONAL. You may ask yourself if you deserve self-care, especially if you have been mean to others or behaved badly. Trust that you are not a bad person and everyone makes mistakes. In fact, the best piece of self-care you can do is to forgive yourself. By forgiving yourself, you will behave in a more forgiving way to others when the situation requires it. Make sure you take responsibility and apologize if necessary, then forgive yourself fully. Learning from mistakes and moving on is far healthier than continually criticizing yourself and feeling forever guilty.

Perhaps you've encountered meanness from someone else, in response to a selfie you posted or the quality of your school work. You deserve emotional self-care from yourself, and to seek out the people around you who really care and love you unconditionally. Those that care about you will always care, no matter what.

KEEP IT PERSONAL

Self-care means different things to different people – it's a very personal thing. For example, some people chant affirmations and mantras to calm themselves, whereas for others hearing and speaking the same words on repeat can make them feel MUCH worse! To create your self-care toolkit, you need to begin by identifying the simple changes you can make to transform your mood and happiness levels. That doesn't mean you can skip homework for gaming – this is not self-care because you will be creating more problems for future you (the one that's sitting in class having to explain why you haven't done it!).

You'll find that your self-care needs will shift constantly according to your current circumstances. Let's imagine it's exam season and you have huge mental challenges ahead. During this time, you might need more sleep and rest, and to eat slow-release energy foods to sustain your concentration. Another example: perhaps you fall out with a good friend and they make you feel bad about yourself. This would be a time to nurture your self-esteem and rebuild your confidence by trying something new or meeting new people.

CHECK IN WITH YOURSELF EVERY DAY

Try to take a few minutes every day to check in with yourself, though preferably not during a lesson. You could even add a reminder to your phone so you do it at a specific time each day. Find a quiet place to sit – maybe your bed or a comfy sofa, preferably undisturbed – and mentally scan your body for discomfort, starting with your toes and going up the body until you reach your head. When you've reached your head, have a dig around in your mind for any niggling worries or concerns. See if you can identify up to three main things that require self-care (either in your mind or your body) and try to think of simple positive changes to transform these thoughts and feelings.

"I'M FEELING LOW AND HAVING DIFFICULTY CONCENTRATING."

Your self-care fix could be something as simple as needing to drink more water so that you're hydrated, or you could think about going for a walk or calling up a friend for a chat.

"I'M CRAVING SUGAR."

When you want to snack on things that aren't good for you it can mean that you're simply bored, or that you're not eating enough of the right things. See how much mess you can create by making your perfect fruit smoothie – it's creative, it's fun and the vitamins will energize your body and mind in the right way.

TAKE A BREATHER

Being constantly connected via social media can feel overwhelming and uncomfortable at times. Even in your free time, you might find yourself scrolling on your phone, keeping up with your feeds and answering messages. One of the simplest and easiest ways to recharge yourself is to switch off the gadgets. (No!!!!!!!) Yes, it might hurt a bit in the beginning, but give it a try for ten minutes at first and then gradually build up to an hour at a time.

WRITE A LIST OF THINGS YOU ENJOY
THAT YOU CAN DO WITH ALL THIS
EXTRA TIME IN YOUR DAY:

_____

_____

_____

_____

_____

_____

_____

LOVE YOURSELF FIRST AND EVERYTHING ELSE FALLS INTO LINE.

Lucille Ball

SAY NO TO BAD FRIENDS

It's not always easy to tell when a friend isn't treating you very well, but it's important that you communicate with someone if you feel your relationship is becoming toxic. If they are really your friend, they will listen.

So what does a bad friend look like? Well, they pressurize you to do things you don't really want to, and we're not just talking about dyeing your hair a weird colour or prank calling your neighbours; this could be drugs, alcohol or sex. Don't let this type of controlling person pull you into the dark. Look out for yourself and ask the question: does this person have my best interests at heart and do they make me happy?

TREAT YOURSELF LIKE
YOUR OWN BEST FRIEND

Be a good friend to yourself, because you are going to be the one that you spend your entire life with and you need to get on, or it's going to be a tough ride.

We all have an inner voice – and, quite often, it seems to spend its time making rude, unhelpful remarks! This is what psychologists call self-talk. When your inner voice is saying a lot of negative things about you, stop for a moment and question whether you would say these things to your best friend. Chances are you would not, because you would never intentionally be unkind to another person. Flipping it in this way might leave you shocked at just how unkind you are to yourself.

Stop calling yourself names or judging every inch of your body. Don't pressure yourself to hang out in certain crowds. Think about you, you there, hello, hi, how are you? Say no, say yes, make your own choices, make mistakes, fall down, get up... ok, you get the gist. And never give up.

You are absolutely worthy of love, especially from yourself.

THE MOST IMPORTANT
RELATIONSHIP
IS THE ONE YOU
HAVE WITH YOURSELF.

Diane von Furstenberg

REFRAME YOUR THOUGHTS

Self-talk is powerful. The kinder you are when speaking to yourself (in your head or out loud) the greater the likelihood that you'll feel good about yourself. When you have a negative thought, don't just accept it; try to reframe it so it has a positive slant. For example, many of us get nervous before a social event with new people and we might say something to ourselves like, "I'm too nervous to do this," which can cripple our confidence and may even prevent us from going. Think about what you could say instead, such as, "I've found these situations to be a little uncomfortable in the past, but I'm strong and I can do this!"

SUPPORT EACH OTHER

This book is primarily about looking after yourself, but feeling good also comes from caring about others. When you're a teen you will form some of the strongest emotional bonds of your life, from friendships to future partners. These relationships play an important role in how you see yourself and will have a strong influence on your overall self-esteem.

Having a support system in place consisting of trusted friends means that you can offload some of your worries and check in with people who are experiencing similar feelings to you; you can be there for them too when they're feeling low.

THERE ARE SO MANY BEAUTIFUL REASONS TO BE HAPPY.

THREE GOOD THINGS

Make a habit of paying three compliments to yourself every day when you get up and look at yourself in the mirror. They don't have to be about physical attributes – especially with your morning hair! – but things that make you think "Yes, I'm alright actually", such as:

"I'M A GREAT LISTENER."

"I'M REALLY GOOD TO HAVE AROUND IN A CRISIS BECAUSE I'M CALM AND METHODICAL."

"I'M A GOOD FRIEND."

These nice compliments will make you feel good all day.

START BY WRITING THREE GREAT
COMPLIMENTS TO YOURSELF HERE:

_____

_____

_____

BECOME COMFORTABLE WITH SAYING "NO"

Saying "no" can be hard. We are conditioned to believe that refusing other people's requests is selfish or rude. We worry we'll appear uncaring or, worse, damage our friendships and relationships with others. But what if, by saying yes, you're risking your own mental and physical health? The sad fact is that, in an effort to be liked, many of us take on far more than we'd like to, without stopping to consider how it might affect us or make us feel. Next time someone asks you for a favour, or to meet up with you, don't agree automatically. If you want to say no, be kind but firm; try saying something like: "Thanks for asking, but I've got other plans at that time." (Note that you don't always have to give a particular reason!) Alternatively, if you aren't confident enough to be so direct, buy yourself time. Saying, "Let me see if I'm free," allows you to step away from the situation and consider how the request will affect you.

FOMO IS A NO GO

Fear of missing out is one of the key factors that can prompt you to do things you don't really like or to overdo it, because who wants to be the sad sack that stayed home and spent the evening scrolling through photos of everyone else having the time of their lives?

To reduce the risk of FOMO, be more discerning about the times that you go out and with whom. Make a mental (or physical) list of the things you really enjoy, so that you can tailor your social life to work for you – without compromise.

CHAPTER 2:

FIND WHAT MAKES YOU HAPPY

> DON'T WORRY, BE HAPPY!
> EMBRACE YOUR WEIRDNESS.
> STOP LABELLING,
> START LIVING.
>
> *Cara Delevingne*

What does being happy mean to you? Does it even exist? This is a question that you might ponder at various stages of your teenage years and beyond, when life feels like it's hitting you in the face with a spade. But help is right here with some simple ways to turn that frown upside down and see life as a wonderful adventure rather than your own private nightmare. This chapter introduces some not-so-wacky concepts to grow your happiness through self-care routines and give your self-esteem and confidence a boost.

HORMONES AND HAPPINESS

First, let's talk about hormones. Whether puberty has already hit hard (see spade analogy on previous page) or you're not quite there yet, hormones play a big part in your happiness levels during your teens. You're not the same as you were when you were a child, and equally, you'll be different again once you become an adult and as your brain develops better coping mechanisms for dealing with strong emotions. This change is due to a tidal wave of hormones flooding your brain. Testosterone rises during puberty for everyone (though generally in smaller quantities in females). This hormone not only plays a role in your physical development, but also helps you to deal with challenging situations. When faced with something upsetting – like getting a bad grade or falling out with a friend – the teenage brain can struggle with processing these feelings and make you feel angrier than you ever thought possible. When this happens, don't beat yourself up, just appreciate that the prefrontal cortex (the bit at the front of the brain just behind your forehead) is still forming. Once developed it will help to keep your moods in check. Everyone goes through this, so just give yourself a break, OK?

GET REAL

IN THIS WORLD NOTHING
CAN BE SAID TO BE CERTAIN,
EXCEPT DEATH AND TAXES...
AND YOUR FAIR SHARE OF
SH*T STORMS.

Benjamin Franklin (mostly)

There are a few more certainties in life than death and taxes, and one of those things is that every now and then – in fact, maybe more often than that – things won't go your way. It's a tough realization, but once you know that this is life's way of knocking off your rough edges and helping you grow, you have the advantage. Yes, you! Resilience will get you through anything – even accidentally posting a picture of your bottom or losing your passport down a train toilet on a gap year to India. Yes, anything! When the sh*t hits, tell yourself, "I'll get through this." And believe it, because you will, and you'll be all the stronger for it.

START THE DAY IN THE BEST POSSIBLE WAY

What's the first thing you do in the morning? Grab your phone to check Instagram? Do a big stretch and have a mental rundown of what's happening today? (You're a future company director if you do!) Do you jump out of bed fully-dressed and race out of the door because you're already late for registration? Or throw the duvet over your head and groan loudly? Or maybe just panic? The way you wake up can set the tone for the entire day, so have a think about how you can do so positively. Treat yourself kindly and begin by acknowledging how you're feeling and say good morning (or afternoon) to yourself. OK, that might feel a bit weird at first, so you could try making a list of three things to be grateful for right now. It could be something super simple, like being grateful for a good night's sleep, or the drink that someone brought for you, or that you have something specific to look forward to today.

These little reminders will put you in the right frame of mind to deal with whatever challenges the day has in store for you.

I'M GRATEFUL FOR

1

2

3

SMILE!

While it doesn't seem very natural to give a big cheesy grin when you're in a bad mood or feeling low, smiling on purpose can actually help to lift your mood and make you feel better. The reason? The very act of smiling alters your brain chemistry, prompting the release of the feel-good neurochemicals: serotonin, dopamine and endorphins. So, even when you're worried, anxious or stressed, try a smile and the good mood may follow. Obviously, there are moments when smiling isn't appropriate – you'll learn those quite quickly.

It's a new day. Count
your blessings, think twice
before you complain, give
more than you ask for, do
what makes you happy
and enjoy life.

Ariana Grande

LAUGHTER

It's said that children laugh over 400 times a day and adults only 15 times a day. So somewhere between being a child and being an adult – when you're a teenager – there clearly isn't much to laugh about. But that needn't be the case! Laughter is a brilliant stress reliever as it boosts energy by releasing extra oxygen into the bloodstream; it also reduces stress hormones and improves memory and creativity, which is why more of it will help you to cope with the everyday demands of being a teen. What's more, sharing a laugh is great for cementing friendships and there's nothing better than having a giggle with your mates. Think of some fun things to turn up the laughter levels: maybe have a games afternoon, a photo booth shoot or just swap clothes!

MY SMILE IS MY FAVOURITE PART OF MY BODY.

Serena Williams

THINK LIKE AN OPTIMIST (EVEN IF YOU'RE NOT ONE)

We all know someone who is endlessly upbeat, and sometimes they can seem pretty annoying when you're feeling weighed down with stress. The thing is, they're not free from worries or self-doubt – we all have a healthy dollop of that to contend with – but they are choosing to be happy despite whatever is going on in their lives. It sounds so simple, but the magical thing about being positive is it's infectious (in a good way!). If you have a happy outlook, you'll start to see a shift in your thought patterns about how you feel about yourself and the world around you. It will also improve your interactions with people – you will become instantly more approachable.

Here are some other tips to help you think like an optimist:

➡ Get moving! It's much harder to feel glum if you're dancing to happy songs or speed walking round the park.

➡ Reward yourself with little treats, just to show your appreciation for the wonderful person that you are.

➡ If you sense a grump coming on, mentally shoo it away and tell it that you haven't got time for it today.

DON'T COMPARE YOURSELF TO OTHERS

This is much easier said than done, especially with the edited highlights of other people's lives constantly flooding onto your phone (not that comparisons are any less hard in real life). Who doesn't look at another person's feeds and wonder how the hell they could ever look as good, or secretly die inside when a friend gets a higher grade in an exam when you worked so hard? It's normal to feel like you're not good enough, but it doesn't feel very nice and it's not good for your self-worth or long-term happiness.

The next time you start to feel small and you believe you don't match up to someone else, make sure you have some self-confidence boosters at the ready. Comparing yourself to others steers you away from looking at all the positive things happening in your life. Write a list of what makes you awesome and read it every time you need a reminder – make it special, embroider it, paint it, laminate it, because YOU ARE AWESOME!

KNOW WHEN IT'S TIME TO TAKE A PAUSE FROM SOCIAL MEDIA

If you regularly feel inadequate after scrolling through social media and your list of "what makes me awesome" isn't hitting the spot, it's time to think about reducing the time you spend online. Some psychologists describe spending too much time on social media as a type of "self-harm", and it's easy to see why. The worst aspect of social media is that it's like being in a popularity contest where you're judged, but you also become very judgemental of others and yourself, too – which can quickly turn toxic and damaging.

There are many great things about social media but try to become more aware of how you are feeling after being online – if you find that you feel bad about yourself and your self-worth has taken a battering, it's time to rethink your relationship with it.

MAKE SURE YOU
ARE HAPPY IN
REAL LIFE AND
NOT JUST ON
SOCIAL MEDIA.

SOCIAL MEDIA AND SELF-CARE

If the previous two tips resonated with you, here are some ideas on how to stay positive and keep a sense of perspective while engaging in social media:

⇒ Try not to reach for your phone as soon as you wake up; instead, focus on you and how you're feeling. If this sounds like a step too far, consider adding your favourite radio station app to your phone so you wake up listening to music, or listen to a podcast. Think about what the day might have in store and mentally prepare yourself for it, rather than falling down a rabbit hole of impossible self-imposed expectations. Every day is a new day, full of infinite possibilities, and you're not going to make the most of life going on around you if you feel rubbish about yourself.

⇒ Switch off notifications to avoid temptation. Consider downloading apps that place limits on your social media access.

⇨ Think before you click "follow". Are their posts inspirational to you or could they be damaging to your health and happiness? Don't "follow" someone just because everyone else seems to – make your own choices and only follow people or companies that add something to your life, rather than suck out the joy.

⇨ If someone follows you, it doesn't mean you have to follow them. If you haven't met them in real life and they're not your friend, you don't owe them a "follow". Consider making your account private to prevent strangers or people you don't get on with following or messaging you.

⇨ Don't eat and scroll, especially if you're prone to snacking; you will end up eating things without even noticing. Plus, it's bad manners!

⇨ Try to go screen-free for an hour before bed and do something nice for yourself like have a bath or read a book.

SELFIES, SELF-CARE AND BODY IMAGE

In your teens, your body and your brain go through big changes. The hormones flooding your body suddenly make you acutely aware and more critical of how you look and increase your awareness and interest in other people's bodies. Teens of all genders who check social media between 50 and 100 times a day are 37 per cent more distressed about their physical appearance and have an increased risk of developing an eating disorder or body dysmorphia.

If you regularly feel low about your body image after browsing online, the first thing to remind yourself is that these images are often digitally enhanced to make them look "perfect" and they do not reflect how people look in real life – just take a walk down your street and you'll see all different shapes and sizes. Nobody is Insta-perfect in real life.

One effective method, recommended by therapists and the patients themselves, to combat negative body image is to find distractions and to engage your mind in activities that absorb you and steer you away from negative thought patterns. This could be learning a musical instrument, painting and drawing, doing puzzles, sport, dance, reading a book or anything else that requires you to focus fully on a task. Spending time with people that make you feel good and that you can have a laugh with is also encouraged – because these people value you for your personality, not your appearance. If you have doubts about this, just write down the nice things people say to you that are not appearance-focused and you will soon see! The directory at the back of this book has information on where to seek support if you feel that negative body image is impacting your life.

Anything is possible when you have the right people there to support you.

Misty Copeland

FIND YOUR TRIBE

The saying goes that it takes a village to bring up a child, but what happens when you're a teenager? The same still applies, but once you've had your first taste of freedom and the bright lights of the more exciting town you might not want to spend all your time in the village. Then what? You find your own group of like-minded people, that's what. Don't be surprised when you start at high school if some of your friends for life from primary school drift away from your orbit and find new friends for life. So will you. People change and that's fine. You will find whole new avenues for making like-minded friends in this bigger, more complex school community. The best way is to say "yes" to invitations and opportunities that come your way, to join clubs and go to meet-ups, whether they're online or in real life.

OPEN UP

If you're low it might seem difficult to start talking to a friend or family member about how you're feeling. However, take comfort in the fact that many people report feeling much better after sharing their thoughts and experiences. If you don't feel up to talking to a friend – either in person or on the phone – why not send them a message to let them know how you're doing?

Teenage life is like a pressure cooker of emotions and responsibilities. It's not a sign of weakness to ask for help – it shows emotional strength and self-love. If you want to seek out someone that can offer advice or just a listening ear to help you make decisions, there are many options open to you. Your school counselling service, your doctor or teen-focused online organizations can help you to reach the right person. Trust that you are never alone and help is always out there. Check out the directory at the back of this book. You are loved and people do care.

VERY LITTLE IS NEEDED TO MAKE A HAPPY LIFE: IT IS ALL WITHIN YOURSELF, IN YOUR WAY OF THINKING.

Marcus Aurelius

WHAT CAN YOU DO FOR YOURSELF RIGHT NOW?

Words can hurt, especially the ones that you say to yourself. They pierce our skin like splinters and can be hard to shift. So, imagine this exercise does the opposite: patting you on the back or planting kisses on your face, whichever you prefer!

Fill in the space on the facing page with positive factual statements about yourself. It can be achievements that you're proud of, talents that you possess, things that you have a passion for or interest in, the way you style your hair, your diplomacy when dealing with difficult people, your amazing talent for mental arithmetic – anything! Keep adding to the page. When every space on the page is covered, get yourself a large poster-size piece of paper, pin it onto your wall and keep adding new things as and when you think of them.

CHAPTER 3:

SELF-CARE FOR MIND AND BODY

> WE EACH HAVE OUR OWN
> FORM OF BEAUTY AND
> THAT'S REALLY SPECIAL.
>
> *Zendaya*

We've already addressed the powerful impact that our perception of our own and others' appearance has on our mental health. The UK mental health charity Mind suggests that taking care of your appearance is a key element when maintaining a positive attitude and self-worth, so in this chapter we are going to look at simple ways to implement a personal grooming self-care routine, and what to do with that fresh crop of follicles – you know what I'm talking about!

GIVE THANKS FOR WHAT YOUR BODY DOES FOR YOU

It's easy to get caught in a negative cycle of focusing on the things that we don't like about our bodies. If this sounds like you, try to look at your body in a different way and appreciate the things that it can do. When you look in the mirror, stand tall and thank your body for the positive things, such as being able to move and twist in order to dance to your favourite music, or write beautiful words, or smell and taste chocolate, or run fast, jump or simply walk. Your body is your vehicle through life and all the things it can do are miraculous. Even when you consider the things that you might consider negatives – like feeling pain, being too thin or not being strong enough – always try to be kind to your body and respect it for just being.

OUT, DAMNED SPOT!

School photo day comes around and three spots appear on your forehead, or worse, on the tip of your nose. Just typical, isn't it? Take a deep breath; it's going to be OK. Just don't squeeze them, however tempting. Skin-coloured concealer might be the quick fix on this occasion, but establishing a really simple skincare routine is the way forward if you want to minimize future breakouts. Nearly everyone experiences spots in their teens (mostly as a result of a hormonal surge) but they can stick around for longer and become more problematic due to other factors, including stress, heavy sweating and humidity. There are preemptive methods you can use to reduce pimples, though. First, let's get down to business and explain how a spot forms. It's all down to your hair follicles, which can get blocked by excess oil (sebum) once it has mixed with dead skin cells.

So, for the most part – unless you have acne or another skin condition – preventing preventing or limiting spots is as simple as keeping your skin clean by using a cleanser (a cream- or oil-based solution, but some people opt for good old-fashioned soap and water) and using an exfoliator (a body scrub, cleanser for the face and a loofah for limbs) once or twice a week to scrub away dead skin. The main takeaway is to wash your face morning and night, and NEVER go to bed with make-up on!

Self-care skin essentials

➡️ **Exfoliating products** – These are often cream- or oil-based solutions that contain granules of some sort – salt, sugar or other natural particles (ensure they are natural, and not plastic microbeads) – that help loosen and remove dead skin cells. Avoid if you have sensitive or broken skin. Use a pumice stone to exfoliate the skin on your feet, and a loofah for your body, but have a soak in the bath beforehand to soften your skin.

➡️ **Cleanser** – This facial care product is used to remove make-up, dead skin cells, oil, dirt and other types of pollutants from your face. It helps to unclog pores and prevent skin conditions such as acne.

➡️ **Concealer** – When matched properly with your skin tone this semi-solid cream will help to hide blemishes. It is often used for smaller areas. If you want to mask redness, a green concealer (made in the colour green, which will neutralize any strong tones) is invaluable.

SKIN TYPE

Before you head to the nearest chemist, you need to figure out your skin type so that you can buy products that are right for you. There's a simple way of telling what skin type you have (apart from the obvious clues). Start by washing your face with a mild soap or cleanser, rinse with lukewarm water and carefully pat dry. After an hour, if you notice you have oil on your nose, forehead and cheeks, you most likely have oily skin. If there's a little shine on just your nose and forehead, you have normal/combination skin. If there is no shine on your face and if when you pull a few facial expressions it feels tight, you have dry skin.

Ethnicity is also a factor in skin type, in that it can determine how your skin reacts to various environmental conditions. For example, though all skin needs to be protected from the sun, darker skin tones have more natural protection from UV rays (and lighter skin tones have less). Research indicates that darker skin is least likely to be irritated when the skin's natural barrier is compromised – for example, during shaving – whereas Asian skin is most easily irritated. You might already know these things from experience, but it's worth keeping in mind when you're considering how best to look after your skin.

Your gender also plays a part in your skin type – male skin is 20 per cent thicker than female skin and has more active sebaceous glands, meaning it's more likely to be oily and prone to spots. So, no matter your gender or skin type, you need to cleanse!

HAIR ON YOUR HEAD

Often, the type of skin you have affects your hair type. If you have dry skin, you probably have dry hair. The same goes for oily skin and oily hair. Different hair types require different products to keep hair in good condition, but the general rule of thumb is to stick to these basic rules:

➡ Keep your hair clean by washing it every couple of days to remove sweat, grime and dead skin. If you have very curly hair, it can be less often.

➡ Use hair care products that complement your hair - so, if you have dry hair, use a shampoo, conditioner and styling products for dry hair, and so on. There is a product out there for every hair type.

- Use an anti-dandruff shampoo at least once a week if you sometimes have a flaky scalp.

- Avoid using heated straighteners, curlers and hairdryers too often as this dries out the natural oils in your hair, which can make it dry and brittle.

- Aim to have a haircut every six weeks to avoid split ends.

- Use a brush or comb both morning and night to avoid knots and to remove stray hairs. There are different grooming products pertaining to your hair type, so do your research. Better still, ask your hairdresser at your next appointment.

- Comb through your hair with a headlice comb once a week - no one is immune!

HAIR THAT'S NOT ON YOUR HEAD

It's time to talk about the fresh crop of follicles that has sprouted on your body, your face and chest. Yep, we're talking facial fuzz, pubic hair, under-arm and chest hair – that's a lot of hair, right? Many young people report their first crop at around age 11. It's like a fluffy badge of honour for reaching puberty! But then fashion trends and beauty influencers tell you to get rid of it, or someone points out your under-arm hair in the changing rooms and tries to shame you for not being silky smooth like them. In some cultures, body hair is seen as an expression of your natural beauty. Like any aspect of you – the physical, mental, emotional or spiritual – deciding on what to do or what not to do is entirely up to you. Don't be forced or pressured into anything you're not happy to do.

There are a number of reasons why you might opt for hair removal. It may be a personal preference and a form of self-expression, or a case of hygiene because body hair can make you sweat more. If you do want to remove some, or all, of your body hair, don't grab the cheap razor on the side of the bath – you need the right tools for the job.

This is not a beauty bible, and there are many ways of removing hair, from waxing and shaving to electrolysis and tweezing. Everyone has an opinion on what works best, so just remember to do whatever feels right for you!

EYEBROWS

It's in your teenage years that you will likely first experience the butt-clenching pain that accompanies tweezing your eyebrow hair. Sorry, it doesn't have to be that bad, but the first time you do it you might wince a teeny bit. If you do choose to pluck your eyebrows, here are a few tips to keep in mind.

➡ Get a face cloth and dampen it with warm water before placing the cloth on your face to soften the skin around your eyebrows, as this will open the pores and make the plucking less painful.

➡ Before you start plucking, you need to find where your eyebrows should end to best suit your face shape. Take a straight object – a pencil is a good choice – and place it vertically against the side of your nose. The point where it reaches your eyebrow is where the eyebrow naturally ends on most people, which is a little past the corner of your eye.

- Brush your brows in the direction that they are growing using either a brow brush or a toothbrush (a cheap one bought specifically for this purpose will do).

- Pluck out the hairs that grow between your brows with tweezers - one hair at a time and as close to the root as possible.

- Trim any extra-long or out-of-place hairs with some small scissors (nail scissors will do).

- Brush and repeat.

- Do not pluck above the brow line as this will upset the natural curve of your brows.

- Pluck the hairs that are growing outside of the main brow area - pull them out in the direction they grow.

- If your skin is a bit red and sore, dab the area with a cool flannel.

STAY FRESH

Let's talk about body odour. Yes, everyone has experienced the familiar *what's that smell?* And then realized it's them. Teens sweat more and this is (once again!) due to your hormones, because they boost the amount of moisture that your sweat glands produce and create body odour. Sweat in itself doesn't cause the smell – it's when the bacteria on your skin mingles with the sweat and your body's natural oils and breaks it down that the whiff is produced. There is a simple self-care routine to help manage this:

➡ The first thing is to wash daily and ideally after sweat-inducing exercise - showering is best (for you and the environment), using an antibacterial shower gel.

➡ Dry yourself thoroughly and apply a deodorant under your arms. Antiperspirant will reduce sweating, but it won't block the odour.

➡ Change your clothes regularly – once a day should be enough – and wear breathable fabrics such as cotton that allow the air to circulate around your body and absorb excess sweat.

➡ Diet can affect body odour, too. Eating spicy food and drinking too much coffee can make it worse – so be moderate with your intake of these.

➡ The increase in sweat and oil production will stabilize by the end of puberty, but if it's affecting your self-esteem, there are many products to try that can be recommended by a pharmacist or doctor.

➡ If you have a menstrual cycle, change your sanitary pad, tampon or menstrual cup regularly throughout your period. Shower daily and keep your pubic area clean with warm water and a mild soap. Don't clean inside your vagina – it is a self-cleaning organ, and using body wash in this area could lead to infection.

STAY FRESH

Fresh breath is vital for oral health and for keeping friends. Here are some tips and quick fixes if you've started the day with a latte or have forgotten to brush your teeth.

⇒ Water – Drinking water literally washes away odour-causing food and bacteria.

⇒ Green tea – Sipping green tea, which contains polyphenols, helps to fight mouth odour.

⇒ Apples – Eating an apple, which also contain polyphenols, can help to neutralize smells.

⇒ Baking soda – Mix a teaspoon in a glass of water (add a drop of peppermint oil if you have some), rinse it around your mouth and spit it out like a mouthwash.

⇒ Lemons – Cut a wedge of lemon, sprinkle a little salt on it and suck on it. You'll have fresh breath, but you might also have watery eyes! (Be aware that too much citric acid is not good for the enamel on your teeth, so this method should be used only in emergencies.)

CHAPTER 4:

FIND YOUR BALANCE

YOU CAN'T HAVE EVERYTHING
YOU WANT, BUT YOU CAN
HAVE THE THINGS THAT
REALLY MATTER TO YOU.

Marissa Mayer

In order to be healthy in mind and body, you need to nourish and exercise mind and body – you know this! As a teen you'll be going through many physical and emotional changes, and these changes need to be supported by a healthy balanced diet, regular physical activity and a good sleep routine. Finding what works for you and your lifestyle will help you to feel strong, empowered and ready to cope with life's challenges (big and small). This chapter offers ways to find what's best for you in order to find balance and feel your best.

EXERCISE TO FEEL GOOD – NOT TO PUNISH YOURSELF

First things first: remember that physical exercise should be fun and something that you enjoy doing. It's not meant to be something to dread, otherwise it's going to be hard to sustain. So, before you sign up to that half marathon in six months' time when you don't enjoy running, take a breath and ask yourself if it's something that you will love or loathe. There are many forms of exercise to try and something to suit all tastes, so the best thing to do is try lots of different types before settling on a few. Luckily, when you're at school or college, you should have free access to different equipment and recreational spaces, with opportunities to join teams and clubs – so spend a bit of time exploring and trying out different options.

HOW MUCH EXERCISE?

In terms of the amount of physical activity you should ideally be doing, experts recommend that teenagers try to incorporate an hour of moderate to vigorous aerobic exercise every day. Strength training exercises and flexibility exercises should also be incorporated a couple of times a week. Aim to spread out the different forms of exercise, and try not to spend long periods of time sitting or lying down in the day.

Aerobic exercise

This can be anything that raises your heart rate and makes you sweat, such as cycling, running, dancing, speed walking or swimming. This form of exercise keeps your heart and lungs healthy and makes you feel stronger and more energized. It also has neurological benefits and has been proven to help cognitive and academic performance. When you feel like you don't have time to exercise – such as when you're preparing for exams – that's when you need aerobic exercise the most, since it releases endorphins (the happy hormone) and cortisol (the stress-reducer), which will help you to feel calm, focused and in control.

Strength training

The testosterone boost that you experience in puberty will help you to build muscle when you perform strength-training exercises (such as lifting weights and bells). This is especially true for males, as they produce more testosterone than females. This type of exercise will also strengthen bones as they continue to grow, as well as improve overall fitness and burn fat.

Flexibility exercises

Flexibility is about the range of motion in your joints and the amount of stretch that your muscles have around these joints when you move. Stretching regularly is really important when you're growing because muscle tissue grows more slowly than bone and this often leads to tightness and body aches. Stretching can alleviate these symptoms and also make you more resistant to sprains and sports-related injuries. Yoga, gymnastics, martial arts and dance are all effective forms of flexibility exercises.

EXERCISE WITH A FRIEND OR IN A TEAM

Everyone struggles to motivate themselves sometimes. A good way of maintaining your exercise routine is to do it with a friend. You can take it in turns to act as coach and cheerleader while keeping it fun for each other – having a laugh while exercising will increase your chances of sticking to it. Team sports are also a great way of cultivating budding friendships and the regime of practice sessions and matches helps to instil healthy exercise habits for the future. Experts have also found that those who regularly participate in team sports are more socially advanced and emotionally intelligent than those that don't, so participating could help you to form more meaningful and mature friendships, be better able to cope with different social situations and work well in a team situation. Never underestimate the importance of being able to get on with others. You will encounter many situations in life when you have to work or socialize with people who have very different views and characteristics to yourself!

The other vital lesson that you learn from being part of a team is that sometimes you will lose, and how you respond to this is all-important. Winning is nice, but the resilience that you learn from losing can be even more valuable as it teaches persistence and that the things which are really worth having are the ones that you have to work hard for.

IS THERE SUCH A THING AS TOO MUCH EXERCISE?

The simple answer is "yes". This is called compulsive exercising and teens can be particularly susceptible due to external pressures to look a certain way and be a certain weight – this applies to all genders. Sometimes it can be hard to recognize this in yourself and that's where it's important to look out for each other, be aware of the signs and seek support when required. Here are the red flags:

⇒ They are making exercise the primary focus, so that it impacts schoolwork and friendships.

⇒ They are constantly checking appearance for signs of weight gain and avoiding eating in front of others.

⇒ They are exercising several times a day, and in secret, such as planking in their bedroom.

⇒ If your inner alarm bell is ringing after reading this list, follow up swiftly by reaching out for support from a trusted adult or your doctor.

A BALANCED DIET

Food is fuel. Eating the right things will benefit your overall health and allow your body to develop and grow properly. A balanced diet will also boost your energy levels and mental function and lower your risk of developing serious illnesses in later life. Out of all the periods in your life, your childhood and teenage years are the most crucial time to learn good eating habits; your body will thank you for it by providing you with vitality and good health.

Eating well doesn't mean you have to say no to the occasional pizza or chocolate bar – all things in moderation are fine. Aim to eat a balance of protein (such as beans, pulses, nuts, fish, tofu and lean meat), carbohydrates (wholegrain bread and pasta, rice and starchy vegetables) and healthy fats (avocados, oily fish, nuts and olive oil), as well as lots of tasty vitamin-rich fruits and vegetables.

BREAKFAST BRAIN FUEL

When you're a teen it's likely that you'll get to pick your breakfast, lunch and snacks during the week, and your dinner will be prepared for you at home. Always eat breakfast. If you're watching your weight, don't skip meals – all this is likely to do is disrupt your metabolism and cause bloating, give you brain fuzz for much of the day and make you feel less able to cope with the day as your body struggles to keep functioning properly. Running on empty feels horrible and the more you do it, the more anxious and out of control you will start to feel, which is not conducive to doing well in exams or in anything.

Opt for slow-release energy foods for breakfast to keep you focused in morning lessons and energized until lunch – in case you don't have time for a snack. Porridge or fortified cereal with milk and fruit is good for essential nutrients such as Vitamin D, iron and calcium. If you have a sweet tooth, a healthy dollop of honey, peanut butter or Nutella on wholegrain toast or on your porridge will hit the spot.

 For the girls

Teen girls can be more susceptible to low iron levels because they lose iron during their period. If you're feeling run down at the same time each month, give yourself an extra boost with breakfast cereals and bread fortified with iron.

SUPER SNACKS

You will get super-hangry – blame those hormones, growth spurts and all that coursework – and that's why it's good to have some snacks on standby. Just a small amount of protein with carbs or fruit and veg will help you to keep going until your next main meal. Here are some ideas to try:

➡ Eggs and soldiers - Dippy eggs are a great source of protein and if you're a gym regular, this simple feast will support muscle growth as well as keep you healthy.

➡ Vegetable sticks and pretzels with hummus - This is another fun food to eat on the go, and it's also very filling and tasty, too.

➡️ Popcorn – Yes, an even more fun snack, and it contains plenty of good fats and energy to keep you going till dinner. Pop on a movie as well.

➡️ Home-made fruit smoothie – These are full of essential vitamins and nutrients.

➡️ A chunk of cheese, a pot of yoghurt or a handful of almonds – You're growing and you need the calcium for strong bones and teeth.

➡️ A bowl of cereal with your choice of milk and fruit on top.

➡️ If you do crave chocolate, have some dark chocolate. It's actually good for you.

FOOD FREEDOM

Lunch is likely to be the only meal you eat away from home, which means for the first time you get to choose what you have. Rather than going all out with processed food and sugary treats, which will make you feel lethargic for the afternoon's lessons as well as generally not being good for you, try to steer towards the healthy options available. Over half of teens take a packed lunch to school these days, and whether you have it made for you or you prepare it yourself, it needs to contain protein, carbohydrates, healthy fats and vitamins. This doesn't have to mean the same boring floppy sandwich day after day – try some of these for size:

→ Change up your sandwich for a bagel or wrap and add your choice of fillings.

→ Buddha bowl - Far from being a religious experience, it's a bowl of colourful and healthy goodies such as rice, vegetables, salad and pulses - anything that you have to hand. This is the tastiest thing around and it's easy to assemble and pack into a reusable lunchbox.

→ Hummus and a selection of foods to dip into it - Pitta bread, crackers, rice cakes and vegetable sticks are all good candidates.

→ Pasta with pesto and extra bits and pieces such as sundried tomatoes and peas.

→ A flask of homemade soup.

STAY HYDRATED

Our bodies rely on having enough water to function properly. Water transports hormones, chemical messages and nutrients to every organ in the body. When we're lacking water, we can start to feel anxious. Dehydration can have similar effects to a panic attack – racing heart, dizziness and a dry mouth – which will certainly hamper your ability to learn and study effectively.

When you're a teen it's recommended that you consume around two litres of water a day (more if you exercise). This can be in the form of food or liquids, such as citrus fruits, soup, milk, vegetable juice and ordinary tap water. Take a water bottle with you to school every day – keep it out on your desk if you can – and try to fill it up two or three times during the school day. Taking regular sips will calm your mind and keep you focused.

BE HEALTHY AND TAKE
CARE OF YOURSELF BUT
BE HAPPY WITH THE
BEAUTIFUL THINGS THAT
MAKE YOU YOU.

Beyoncé

SLEEP – FOOD FOR THE BRAIN

You might find that your sleep patterns become more irregular as a teenager, as it's common to want to go to bed much later than you ever have before – even if that means you have to muddle through with zombie-brain the next day. Experts say that teens need around eight to ten hours sleep a night to function well in the day, but many don't get this amount due to the circadian rhythms that shift when you become a teenager – so that you naturally fall asleep later and get up later. Regularly failing to get enough sleep can lead to sleep disorders such as insomnia (resulting in low mood and poor concentration) and contribute to skin conditions, such as acne. Sleep might not be exciting in itself, but it's vital to your health, well-being and happiness. Here are some ways to make it easier to nod off:

→ Make your bedroom a sleep sanctuary; a tidy, fresh and clean room will encourage more restful sleep.

→ Establish a bedtime routine and try to stick to it, such as taking a shower, then reading a chapter of a book. These regular activities will become signals to your body that it's time for bed, meaning you will find it easier to fall asleep and feel refreshed in the morning.

→ The few hours before you go to bed should be reserved for restful and calming activities – this means no homework or cramming for the exam the next day – and try to avoid screens before bed, too, so you don't end up scrolling till the small hours!

→ Avoid stimulants before bed, such as caffeinated drinks and sugary food – this is likely to make you wide-awake and buzzing!

→ Try writing down all the things spinning around in your mind, no matter how silly they look on paper. That way, you can safely forget about them for as long as you need to rest and recharge.

SELF-CARE BEDTIME CHECKLIST

This checklist is by no means definitive and it will be different from one person to the next. Use the prompts and adapt the checklist so it works well for you. Once you have a good bedtime routine in place, try to keep to it to ensure good sleep every night.

De-stress

⇒ Write down anything that's on your mind

⇒ Chat with a friend

⇒ Do something calming that you enjoy for half an hour

⇒ Have a decaffeinated drink

⇒ Make sure your room is tidy and your bed is fresh and inviting

⇒ Turn down the lights after 9.30 p.m.

Make preparations for the next day

⇨ Prepare clothes/uniform and pack bag

⇨ Check diary or any notifications for the next day

⇨ Charge phone and place on "silent mode"

⇨ Set alarm

Get ready for sleep

⇨ Wash and change

⇨ Stretch/meditate

⇨ Read a chapter of a book or listen to nature sounds or calming music

⇨ Make your room as dark as possible, or wear a sleep mask

⇨ Relax

AND IF YOU REALLY CAN'T SLEEP...

Don't beat yourself up if you can't nod off. As a teen, you're far more likely to recover quickly from tiredness than, say, your parents. You can try doing one of your calming activities, such as reading or doodling for a bit, but try not to reach for your phone – the blue light from your phone will interfere with your sleep patterns as it disrupts the production of the sleep hormone, melatonin. Another way to relax your body into sleep is to have a drink of water, tuck yourself in, check you're warm enough, close your eyes and slowly tense and release your muscles one after the other working up your body, from your toes to your head. This technique is called progressive muscle relaxation, and it's proven to be an effective way to soothe your body and relieve stress. If you regularly struggle to get to sleep, try speaking to your doctor, as it might be a symptom of depression.

I LOVE TO SLEEP. I'D SLEEP ALL DAY IF I COULD.

Miley Cyrus

CHAPTER 5:

ACHIEVE YOUR POTENTIAL

> BELIEVING IN YOUR OWN
> SELF-WORTH IS ESSENTIAL
> TO ACHIEVING YOUR
> FULL POTENTIAL.
>
> *Sheryl Sandberg*

Let's get down to business – school is a big deal. The choices you make now and the exam results that you achieve can have some bearing on your immediate future, but remember you are not defined by these exams. The stress that this period can generate can feel overwhelming at times, but it needn't be. This chapter offers ways to keep your stress levels in check by adopting some simple but effective relaxation techniques, to make sure life remains enjoyable.

TRY MEDITATION TO SETTLE EXAM NERVES

We've already touched upon progressive muscle relaxation for helping you get to sleep, but there are other forms of meditation to try that could help you to feel more peaceful and in control during your exams. Guided visualization can be a useful technique to try during exam season, especially if just being in the the exam room makes you. If you have a specific goal in mind – in this case acing your exams – the idea is to sit in a calm and quiet space, close your eyes and slowly visualize the situation, trying to be as detailed as you can be. Think of details as specific as the pencil case that you will bring and the questions

on the paper, even the weather outside, allowing the scene and the positive outcome that you desire to be as real as possible in your mind's eye. Take deep breaths, imagining yourself breathing in calm and breathing out stress. Slowly open your eyes and keep breathing in calm and breathing out stress. Practise this method a few times in the run up to your exams and when it comes to exam day, try the breathing technique for a minute or two before you begin.

WHAT IF MY MIND GOES BLANK?

If you've had a bad exam experience where your mind has gone blank or you studied the wrong part of the syllabus, it can make you anxious for the next exam. It can help to prepare by doing practice papers or past papers which are available online, and if you are still worried, speak to your course tutor for guidance and support; they can help you make the process less scary by talking you through what to expect on the day and even show you the exam hall beforehand. It's completely normal and natural to experience exam nerves, but keep reminding yourself of the time and effort you have put into studying and this should help you to feel more confident.

Grounding exercise

If your mind starts to spin at any point in the exam, here's a simple mindfulness exercise to help you settle your thoughts and regain a sense of calm. It's called the 5, 4, 3, 2, 1 exercise (for obvious reasons!). Try to learn it off by heart and practise it throughout your studies so you've trained your mind to do it easily:

- **5** - Look for 5 different objects. Notice their shape. Are they curved or angular?

- **4** - Touch 4 different things. Notice their texture. Are they rough or smooth?

- **3** - Listen for 3 different sounds. Are they soft or sharp?

- **2** - Smell 2 different aromas. Are they sweet or pungent? (LOL)

- **1** - Think of 1 wonderful thing about you.

SHARE THE LOAD

As with maintaining an exercise regime, it can help to have a friend on board for a revision regime, especially if they're on the same course as you, as you can quiz each other and discuss things that you're not sure about. Studying together can also help motivate you to see the end goal and how doing well in the exams will benefit you and boost your sense of self-worth. Another positive aspect of having a study buddy is that you can have a debrief after each exam to ease worries about certain questions that might have proved tricky.

Don't compare

Everyone has differing study and revision patterns (and varying energy levels, too), so don't panic if you hear that someone else has done more preparation than you. Bear in mind that people like to exaggerate these things to give themselves a boost rather than to knock others' confidence.

DON'T STOP PLAYING

It's easy to put fun stuff on the back burner when you're revising or in the middle of exam season, but it's more important than ever! Like meditation and exercise, moving around and burning off nervous energy will help you to focus on your studies and remain calm during exams. Every forty minutes to an hour, give yourself a break from revision and go and do something fun and active for 15 minutes that requires you to think of nothing else but that activity. See this as self-care for your mind and an opportunity to clear your head and step outside of your studies to find perspective. Try some of these – one in each 15 minutes of play – and tick them off when you've achieved them. Then add your own ideas to the list.

- Learn three tricks with a yo-yo
- Do a trick on a skateboard
- Juggle with three pieces of fruit
- Build the tallest sandwich
- Make the most inventive smoothie
- Stand on your head
- Do the crab
- Lie on the grass and count the number of birds that fly overhead
- Sing your favourite song to the nearest person

LEARN TO STOP WORRIES FROM OVERWHELMING YOU

Wouldn't it be great if you could scrunch up your worries between your fingers and flick them into the bin? Well, it's not quite that easy, but there are ways to manage worries while they're still in their infancy so that they're easier to eliminate before they start to snowball. Worries can be sorted into two categories – things you can control and things you can't. The sorts of worries that you can't control are things like other people's opinions or actions, news events or the weather. The worries that you can control become much easier to manage if you have a strategy in place to deal with them. Psychologists use a practice called cognitive behavioural therapy (CBT) to help break the cycle of worry by derailing the same negative thought processes. See how you can break down your worries into simple steps, for example:

TALK TO MY FAVOURITE GROWN-UP

SMILE

CHALLENGE EACH PIECE ONE BY ONE

MY WORRIES

PAUSE

ALLOW THE FEELING

TAKE MINDFUL BREATHS

BREAK DOWN THE WORRY INTO SMALLER PIECES

CREATE YOUR OWN EXAM DAY SELF-CARE CHECKLIST

First of all, prepare this in advance and see it as an important part of your exam revision. Studying the subject matter is only part of the job; the other part is mental preparation, so that you are calm and in control of your nerves. Break the process up into a simple timeline starting with the day before, then the evening before and bedtime, then the morning and finally the exam. Here's an example:

Day before

➡ Read through revision notes for no more than an hour.

➡ Remember 15 minutes of fun (see page 106)!

➡ Talk through any worries about the exam questions with your study buddy or parent/carer.

- Plan your route to the exam hall, set your alarm, get pencil case, exam forms, snacks and clothes ready.

- Use self-care bedtime checklist (see page 94).

Morning of exam

- Eat a healthy, nutritious breakfast (see page 84).

- Breathe in calm and breathe out worry (see page 101).

- Begin the exam, take a breath or use your mindfulness exercise if you feel worried (see page 103).

After the exam

- Have a snack (see page 86).

- Debrief with a friend (see page 104).

- Reward yourself with an activity that you enjoy.

- Rest.

- Prepare for the next day's exam.

Each time we face our fear, we gain strength, courage and confidence in the doing.

Theodore Roosevelt

CHAPTER 6:

SELF-CARE FOR FUTURE YOU

> MY INTEREST IS IN THE FUTURE BECAUSE I AM GOING TO SPEND THE REST OF MY LIFE THERE.
>
> *Charles Kettering*

You've made it to the final chapter. This one is about looking to the future and putting into place some self-care and self-preservation practices while you're a teen that you can carry through to adulthood. It's not as heavy as it sounds, promise! This chapter is about growing your self-worth, standing up for your values and being your true self. The next few years are like those giant first leaps on the moon – they are the first steps to being an independent, resilient, freethinking grown-up.

TRUST YOURSELF

You've come so far in such a short time, and you should be proud of this. We all have wobbles of confidence – *Am I good enough? Am I ready for this?* Learning to trust yourself and your decision-making will give you the confidence to do anything you set your mind to.

Try asking your intuition for guidance on small decisions first: almond croissant or plain? Jeans or shorts? Music or a podcast?

Don't overthink it, just tune in to that wise, quiet voice inside you and make a choice. Making decisions based on intuition isn't as woo-woo as it sounds. Studies have found that intuition is based on your brain processing information that has not yet made it to your conscious awareness, in order to keep you safe. Once you start listening to and trusting your gut feeling, you'll be able to sense it more clearly.

OWN YOUR MISTAKES BUT ONLY APOLOGIZE WHEN YOU NEED TO!

These two things require a level of maturity that even some adults don't possess. Having these skills in your arsenal will show you have an equal respect for yourself and others.

Try to get out of the habit of saying "sorry" for things that don't require an apology. Swap "I'm sorry" for "thank you". For example, instead of "Sorry for bothering you" try "thank you for listening" ... it's so much more positive. Only apologize when you have something to apologize for. If and when you do mess up, apologize sincerely and make amends.

You might wonder how cutting down on your "sorrys" can help. Try looking at it this way: when you say "sorry", you're drawing attention to a perceived failing in yourself. When you say "thank you", you're showing appreciation for the kindness or generosity the other person has shown you.

HANG OUT WITH THE OLDS

Really? Yes, really. Parents know stuff, and they might seem cripplingly embarrassing in any given social situation (and out of touch with gender pronouns and TikTok challenges), but you're stuck with them, so you might as well get on with them. Underneath that slightly wrinkled exterior is someone not dissimilar to you, who has experience of all the things you are going through – and they can learn from you too! They might struggle with predictive text when responding to your messages and pack you off with an extra jumper when you go to a party in case you get cold – and don't even mention the dancing – but they know what it's like to revise (or not) for exams, to have their heart broken, to fall out with friends and make new ones. You might find you have more in common than you ever realized! And keeping the lines of communication open and sharing feelings will help them to help you when you really need them.

STOP NEGATIVITY
IN ITS TRACKS

Our surroundings and the people who populate our lives affect our mindset. Remove negative influences, people and ideas from your attention and you'll find that negative thoughts are easier to control.

Unfollow any social media account that brings up feelings of inadequacy, guilt or anxiety in you. Don't waste time finishing books you're not enjoying. Listen exclusively to music that makes you want to sing along or dance around the house. Fill your environment with beauty, lightness and joy and you'll start to feel the effect on your outlook.

ASSERT YOUR BOUNDARIES

Boundaries are about owning your responsibilities and letting go of the things you aren't responsible for. Here are some golden rules to help you set and assert your boundaries:

- You can't fix others
- You can say no
- You don't need to be understood or agreed with
- You are allowed to feel what you are feeling
- If it feels wrong, don't do it

Setting boundaries can be intimidating if it's a new concept for you. Trust your own mind and understand that if someone reacts with anger, manipulation or offense to your boundaries, their reaction is their own responsibility, not yours.

BUILD YOUR OWN SELF-CARE KIT

It's time to create your own self-care kit. We are all different and no two self-care kits will be the same. Be mindful of meeting all your well-being needs – physical, mental and emotional. You might want to tailor it to your present needs, say, if you're starting a new holiday job or you're taking an exam. Preparing your self-care kit shows kindness to yourself and provides you with a feeling of stability and control, no matter what life holds for you.

SELF-CARE KIT

PHYSICAL

_____

MENTAL

_____

EMOTIONAL

_____

THE LAST WORD

Hopefully this book has opened your eyes to your inner strengths and the importance of looking after yourself.

Always remember:

⇒ There's only one of you – treat yourself as the unique, precious and valuable person that you are.

⇒ You are the most important person in your life, and you deserve to have your needs met.

⇒ Give yourself permission to pause and take a breath.

⇒ Harness the power of "no".

⇒ Tune into your needs and respond to them kindly.

⇒ You can never show too much compassion for yourself.

⇒ Your weight – or how you look – is not your worth.

⇒ The way you speak to yourself matters.

⇒ Self-love and self-care are unconditional.

DIRECTORY

General health and well-being

- actionforchildren.org.uk
- childrenssociety.org.uk
- mentalhealth.org.uk
- nhs.uk
- nspcc.org.uk
- youngminds.org.uk
- who.int
- womenforwomen.org

Eating disorders

➡ nhs.uk

➡ beateatingdisorders.org.uk

➡ seedeatingdisorders.org.uk

➡ nationaleatingdisorders.org

Depression/anxiety

➡ camhs.elft.nhs.uk

➡ childline.org

➡ mind.org.uk

➡ youngminds.org.uk

Substance abuse

➡ mind.org.uk

➡ talktofrank.com

➡ youngminds.org.uk

If you're interested in finding out more about our books, find us on Facebook at **Summersdale Publishers** and follow us on Twitter at **@Summersdale**.

www.summersdale.com